DALI

THE GREAT ARTISTS COLLECTION

MASON CREST

Contents

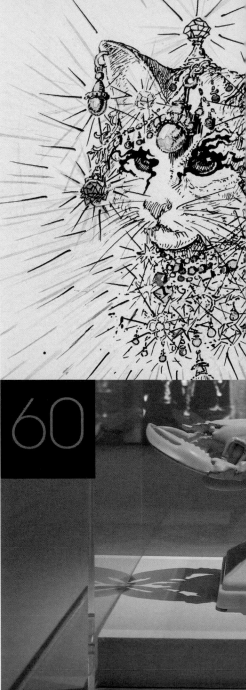

2

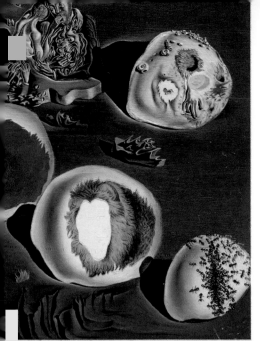

*Great Works order is alphabetical where possible.

DALI

Mason Crest
450 Parkway Drive, Suite D
Broomall, PA 19008
www.masoncrest.com

©2016 by Mason Crest, an imprint of National Highlights, Inc.

Printed and bound in the United States of America.

10 9 8 7 6 5 4 3 2 1

Cataloging-in-Publication Data on file with the Library of Congress.

Series ISBN: 978-1-4222-3256-9
Hardback ISBN: 978-1-4222-3258-3
ebook ISBN: 978-1-4222-8535-0

Written by: Jessica Toyne

Images courtesy of PA Photos and Scala Archives

"Have no fear of perfection – you'll never reach it."
Salvador Dali

Introduction

(AP/AP/Press Association Images)

■ **ABOVE:** Salvador Dali pictured in a typically eccentric pose, he was well known for his trademark mustache.

During a long and illustrious career, Salvador Dali produced more than 1,500 paintings, alongside a great number of drawings, illustrations, lithographs, designs for theater sets, sculptures, and movies. He was also a renowned photographer and fashion designer, noted for his trademark mustache and eccentric forays into the world of Surrealism. The Spanish artist was a great believer in symbolism, and his hallmark "soft watches" are synonymous with his works. As Dali watched a runny piece of Camembert on a hot sunny day, he found his thoughts turning to Einstein's theory that time is relative and, therefore, not fixed. He began to reject the idea that time was rigid and used the soft watches as a way of expressing his own beliefs. The elephant and the rhinoceros are also recurring themes in Dali's work. The rhino, interestingly, symbolized the Virgin Mary for Dali. While soft watches first appeared in one of the artist's most famous works, *The Persistence of Memory* (1931), the elephant was introduced in 1944 in *Dream Caused by the Flight of a Bee around a Pomegranate One Second before Awakening.* Dali remained committed to the influences he gained, and he pushed his own creativity

■ **ABOVE:** Salvador Dali's and Edward James's *Lobster Telephone* is seen at the Surreal Things exhibition at London's Victoria and Albert Museum.

to the limit in his pursuit of what would make him unique as an artist. Other animals are also prevalent in Dali's work, including snails – to depict the human head – ants, portraying death and decay, and locusts to depict fear. He also used the egg as a form of symbolism to portray love and hope. The egg appears in paintings such as *The Metamorphosis of Narcissus* and *The Great Masturbator*.

He was fascinated by quantum mechanics, which celebrated their birth in the 20th century, and he was inspired by breakthroughs in new science. Two of his most popular works were *Lobster Telephone* and *Mae West Lips Sofa*, which he worked on in collaboration with his patron, wealthy art collector and Surrealist artist, Edward James.

Dali was renowned for his pieces that had strong sexual connotations and was convinced there was a close relationship between food and sex. The jewels he created are intricate and exquisite, while his contributions to theater and movies are highly regarded. He was particularly fascinated by dreams and the distortion to reality that they could bring. He ventured into the world of fashion with Italian designer Schiaparelli when he worked on a white dress with lobster print, a shoe-shaped hat, and a belt with lips for the buckle. He also designed perfume bottles and

object d'art, as well as a creation entitled "Costume for the Year 2045," with Christian Dior. He collaborated with other photographers, such as Beaton, Halsman, and Man Ray, photographing nature as well as more unusual subjects, including a bucket of water. While Dali married Gala, his favorite muse, he was also known to have had affairs with younger muses, including Amanda Lear and Isabelle Collin Dufresne, who both went on to have successful careers in the arts. Isabelle, also known as Ultra Violet, went on to become Andy Warhol's muse. He in turn was inspired by Dali. Yet, Dali struggled with physical relationships. It is said that despite the fact he was married to Gala for 48 years, he made love to her only once. The rumor was that Dali found horror in the female anatomy. He was more comfortable with the male body, but still shied away from active physical contact, although there are stories of various sexual acts with men and women. Dali was always accompanied by his Russian wife, and he conquered the way in which the world perceived itself with his extraordinary works of art. When Dali was alive, the tiny village of Port Lligat, close to Cadaqués on Spain's northeastern coast, was a place for "pilgrims." His architectural achievements include his house in Port Lligat, as well as his theater-museum:

Teatro Museo, in Figueres. His literary works are noted and his graphic arts, in which he worked extensively, are highly revered. Politics played a prominent role in his life and his emergence as an artist. He had embraced both anarchism and Communism and had an allegiance to the Dada art movement. This changed in later life, and in 1970, he declared himself an anarchist and monarchist. He refused to become embroiled in politics surrounding the two World Wars, but in the late 1940s he showed some support for Francisco Franco.

Some areas of Dali's life were far too perverse and complex for some of his contemporaries, including George Orwell, who once described the artist as: "an admittedly good draughtsman…[but] a disgusting human being." It is cited that Gala had numerous affairs throughout her marriage to Dali – often with his blessing – and was often cruel to him. However, whether Dali had a "warped" view of the world, and whether or not he was "disgusting," he possessed an almost genius creative flair that was supported and nurtured by Gala – he was obsessed with chastity and virginity, and although there were reports of one illegitimate child in 2008, the fact that it is thought he only participated in full sex twice or three times in his life would make this unlikely. Dali was a highly revered and eccentric artist who opened the door to a level of creativity that the world had never seen before. His legacy will endure.

- **ABOVE:** Dali pictured with his wife, Gala, 1955.

- **BELOW:** Dali's house in Port Lligat was decorated with huge concrete eggs.

(Roland Holschneider/DPA/Press Association Images)

Dali
A Biography

(Mary Evans/Epic/Tallandier)

■ **ABOVE: Dali pictured as a young child.**

Salvador Dali was born on May 11, 1904, in Figueres, Girona, Spain. Nine months before he was born, his older brother, born in October 1901, had died of gastroenteritis. In 1908, the same year his sister, Anna Maria, was born, Dali found himself at the local state primary school where his father, Salvador Dali Cusi, and his mother, Felipa Domenech Ferres, had enrolled him. Things did not quite work out as planned and, in 1910, Dali Senior moved his son to the Immaculate Conception – a Hispano-French school in Figueres where he began learning French. Dali's father, a lawyer and notary, was strict in comparison to his mother, who encouraged her son's artistic talents. However, he was also on the receiving end of some fairly difficult family beliefs. At the age of five, Dali was

■ **ABOVE:** The Municipal Theater, at which Dali studied, later became known as the Dali Theater-Museum.

taken by his parents to his brother's grave and told that he was the reincarnation of their oldest son, also named Salvador. Later in his works, Dali would incorporate the image of his dead older sibling. By the age of 12, Dali had discovered Impressionism.

This came as a result of the young boy's time spent with the Pichot family at the Moli de la Torre estate in Cadaqués. Around this time, in 1916, Dali continued his studies – which had been mediocre to this point – at Marist Brothers' School. He also began to study under Juan Nunez at the Municipal Drawing School, and three years later took part in a local exhibition at the Municipal Theater (later to become the Dali Theater-Museum). The year was 1919 and, along with some school friends, he founded *Studium* magazine, as well as starting a personal diary entitled *My Personal Impressions and Private Memories*. As his interest in art grew, Dali Senior consented to his son studying in Madrid at the Fine Arts School, in order that he could qualify as a teacher. The following year, in 1921, Dali's mother died and his father married his aunt, Cataline Domenech Ferres. It was a difficult time for Dali, who adored his mother; however, he was not upset by his

■ **RIGHT:** Federico Garcia Lorca pictured with Dali, c. 1925.
■ **BELOW:** Real Academia de Bellas Artes de San Fernando, Palacio de Goyeneche, Madrid, Spain.

(Mary Evans/Epic/PVDE)

(Public Domain)

je ne vois pas la

cachée dans la forêt

■ **ABOVE:** The main representatives of the Surrealist movement c. 1927: Maxime Alexandre, Louis Aragon, André Breton, Luis Buñuel, Jean Caupenne, Salvador Dali, Paul Éluard, Max Ernst, Marcel Fourrie, Camille Goemans, René Magritte, Paul Nougé, Georges Sadoul, Yves Tanguy, André Thiron, Albert Valentin. This photomontage was published in *La Revolution Surrealiste*, No. 12, in December 1929.

father's remarriage, as he had a great deal of love and respect for his mother's sister, Cataline.

In 1922, Dali won the University Vice-Chancellor's prize for his work, *Market*, which was exhibited at the Students' Original Art Works Competition, held in Barcelona. Back in Madrid, he attended the Real Academia de Bellas Artes de San Fernando, a painting, sculpture, and engraving school, where he made friends with a group of likeminded people. Here, Dali began to become increasingly aware of his own eccentricity. He had long hair and sideburns and chose to wear a coat, stockings, and knee-brooches. Despite his unconventional demeanor, he made friends with the likes of Pepin Bello, also an artist, Luis Buñuel, a writer, and Federico Garcia Lorca, a playwright, with whom there was a mutual passion. By now, Dali was experimenting with Cubism and was gaining a reputation as a promising artist.

He was, unfortunately, expelled in 1923 after being accused of leading a student protest against painter Daniel Vazquez Diaz, and he returned to study under Juan Nunez who taught him the technique of etching. In 1924, he exhibited at the Iberian Artists Society in Madrid. He also illustrated his first book, *Les Bruixes de Llers*, written by his school friend, and poet, Climent.

(AP Photo)

■ **ABOVE:** André Breton, poet and essayist credited with the founding of Surrealism in literature and art, shown in 1962.

■ **BELOW:** Max Ernst and Paul Éluard with Gala, skiing in Austria, 1922.

(Mary Evans/Epic/Tallandier)

14

(Mary Evans / Everett Collection)

■ **ABOVE:** **Salvador Dali, photographed by Carl Van Vechten, November 1939.**

Dali decided not to return to the Academia de San Fernando and, in 1926, participated in several exhibitions, both in Madrid and Barcelona. This was the same year that he made his first trip to Paris, where he met Pablo Picasso. Picasso had already heard favorable reports of the young Spanish artist. Dali left Paris for Spain, and after an intense period concentrating on his paintings – which included a number of works influenced by Picasso and Joan Miro – he held a sole exhibition (the second for Dali) at Galeries Dalmau in Barcelona, where his first clear influences of Surrealism were beginning to surface. Following this, in 1927, Dali was required to carry out his military service at Sant Ferran Castle, Figueres. Over the next year or so, along with others, he published the Catalan Anti-Artistic Manifesto, (the *Yellow Manifesto*), which mounted a scathing attack on conventional art.

Some of the influences that Dali favored in the 1920s would remain within his works for the rest of his life, and it was at this point, influenced by Diego Velázquez, the 17th-century Spanish master, that he grew his trademark flamboyant mustache.

By 1929, Dali was back in Paris and met André Breton – the leader of the Surrealist movement – and his cohorts for the first time. It was also around this time that the movie, *Un Chien andalou*, was released and shown in the city. It was a collaboration with Buñuel, where Dali's main contribution was to help write the script. This particular year was an inspiring time of new beginnings for Dali, who also met his most influential muse and future wife, Gala. Born into a family of Russian intellectuals, Elena Ivanovna Diakonova, more simply known as Gala, was sent to a sanatorium in Switzerland in 1912 to recover from tuberculosis. It was here that she met Surrealist poet, Paul E. Éluard. The couple married in Paris when both were 22, during the midst of the First World War, in 1917. A year later, the couple's daughter, Cecile, was born, but Gala wasn't a maternal woman and the child was often ignored and neglected. Gala became involved in the Surrealist movement alongside her husband, and for a time, the couple lived in a ménage a trois with Max Ernst. They visited Spain, and it was here that Dali and Gala quickly developed a relationship that would lead to an affair. Despite the fact she was 10 years older, Dali was infatuated with Gala, although the fact she was married did cause him immense angst. Gala continued to be close to Éluard after their marriage broke up.

Dali had been heavily influenced by Surrealism since 1927 and, in 1929, he officially joined the Surrealist group in Paris. He was widely revered for his paranoiac-critical method – a creative process developed by him and

(Mary Evans/Andreu Bonet/Iberfoto)

■ **ABOVE: A monument of Dali next to the beach in Cadaqués, Spain, where he lived for many years.**

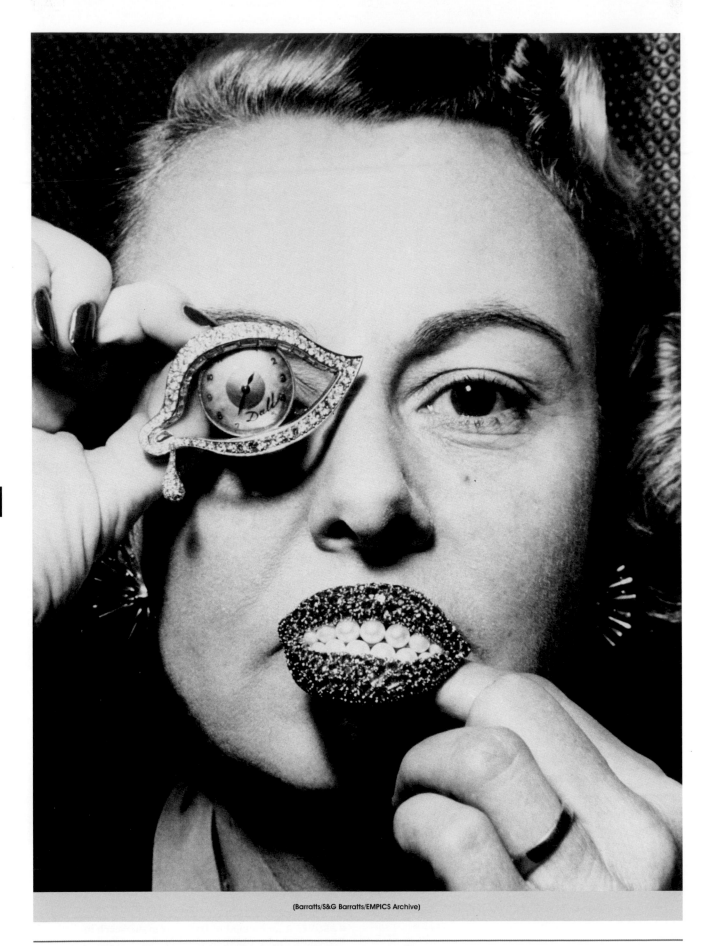

■ **ABOVE:** Watches were to become a trademark of Dali's. Here is a watch in the shape of an eye surrounded by diamonds and rubies. © Salvador Dali, Fundació Gala-Salvador Dalí, DACS, 2013.

used in many of his works that interprets unconscious thoughts into visual illusions. However, while his career went from strength to strength, Dali's private life was to be confronted by his father, who greatly disapproved of his son's relationship with the older, married, Gala. He saw Dali's connections to the Surrealists as a bad influence. Things came to a head when Dali exhibited *Sacred Heart of Jesus Christ* in Paris, which included an inscription about spitting on his mother's portrait for fun. Dali Senior demanded that he recant immediately, but his son refused, and having been thrown out of his father's home and told he would be disinherited, bought a fisherman's cabin in Port Lligat, close to Cadaqués, in the summer of 1930. Dali had been able to do this with the help of Lidia Noguer i Sabà, the daughter of a woman known as Sabana who was regarded as one of the last witches of Cadaqués.

Lidia ran a boarding house for some years and played host to Picasso and Puig i Cadafalch. In 1904, the year of Dali's birth, she had Eugeni d'Ors, the intellectual, to stay for a short time. It led Lidia to develop an obsession with d'Ors, and when he wrote *La Ben Plantada* seven years later, she immediately identified with the protagonist, which it was claimed, finally drove her literally mad. Everything that d'Ors wrote resulted in reams of letters from Lidia to the author, and seven years after her death, d'Ors began to take notice and returned to Cadaqués in order to write a book, *La Verdadera Historia de Lidia de Cadaqués*. Here, he asked Dali to illustrate the work. For his part, Dali had been intending to write his own book about Lidia and was enthused by the idea of illustrating d'Ors's work – Dali had had a friendship with Lidia for many years and had an acute fondness for her.

In 1929, having been thrown from his father's home, it was Lidia who sold him the cabin in which her two sons had previously stored their equipment. It was a special place for Dali and Gala, and was their sanctuary at the start of their relationship. It would become their sanctuary again when they returned from the United States in 1948. Today, it is part of the "Dali triangle."

Dali Senior finally relented about his son's relationship with Gala. It was 1931 when the artist produced one of his most famous works, *The Persistence of Memory*, which included, for the first time, the soft, melting pocket watches with which he would become synonymous. The interpretation given by many for these trademark watches is that Dali rejected time was rigid. Meanwhile, after five years of living together, Dali and Gala were married in a civil ceremony in 1934 – a Catholic ceremony came later in 1958. Gala would inspire Dali's works and she was his

(Mary Evans/Epic/PVDE)

■ ABOVE: A unique image of Dali.

(AP Photo)

The Museum of Modern Art

favored muse, but she was also his business manager. It appears that she tolerated the younger women in Dali's life. Perhaps she was secure in her own relationship and fully aware of the acceptability of the situation in the circles in which they moved. His paintings of Gala were always beautiful and sympathetic, even as the couple aged, and their complex, yet loving, relationship would endure.

The year of the couple's marriage was also the year that Dali was introduced to America by Julien Levy, art dealer and New York gallery owner, who held an exhibition of the artist's works, including *Persistence of Memory*. Dali found himself an instant success, and he and his wife were openly accepted in American high society. However, when they appeared at a party dressed as the Lindberg baby and his kidnapper, the ensuing outrage in the press saw the couple apologize. This apology led to the Surrealist movement being angry with Dali for apologizing for a Surrealist act. While many Surrealists were increasingly associated with politics to the left, Dali insisted that art could remain apolitical. It was his refusal to denounce Fascism that made it impossible for the Surrealists to associate with Dali any further, and he was formally expelled from the group. Dali continued unabated and unperturbed by their actions, and in 1936, took part in the London International Surrealist Exhibition where he gave a lecture dressed in a diving suit and helmet. That same year, Dali exhibited at the Museum of Modern Art in New York, but became more noted for the fact that he accused Joseph Cornell of stealing his movie when *Rose Hobart* was premiered at Levy's gallery. Dali knocked the projector over in anger in the middle of the movie. It would not be the last time that the eccentric Spaniard accused someone of "stealing" his ideas. For two years London patron, Edward James, a wealthy art collector who bought many of the artist's works and helped raise his profile in the art world, supported Dali financially. James collaborated with Dali on *Lobster Telephone* and *Mae West Lips Sofa*. Dali associated with Sigmund Freud, and was invited to spend time at the home of Coco Chanel on the French Riviera. Many of the works he created while in France were later exhibited at Levy's gallery in New York. However,

■ LEFT: This is an exterior view of the Museum of Modern Art, II West 53rd Street in New York, where Dali exhibited in 1936.

(AP Photo)

■ **ABOVE:** Salvador Dali is seen in New York, 1942.

(AP Photo)

■ **LEFT:** Helena Rubinstein poses beside her portrait, painted by Salvador Dali, in her art gallery in New York, 1950. The oil painting is signed by her friend Dali and dated 1946.

■ **BELOW:** Resting his chin on the handle of his cane, Dali studies an exhibit of contemporary Greek art in New York, 1956.

21

(ROBERT KRADIN/AP/Press Association Images)

(PA Photos)

■ **ABOVE:** This statue forms part of the Dali Universe exhibition, dedicated to one of the greatest Surrealist artists of the 20ᵗʰ century, at County Hall, London.

(PA Photos)

■ **LEFT:** Dali unveils one of his new paintings, 1975.

Dali's former Surrealist friends, particularly Breton, began to berate him for the commercialization of his work, and while it's true that Dali thought himself a genius, and made money from his work, the fact that the movement that had so highly revered him should begin to talk about him as if he were dead, was an unfair and cruel turn of events. Dali was anxious to become rich and famous, but his works continued to develop and demand his efforts, just as they always had done.

When war broke out, Dali and Gala moved to the United States. They arrived in 1940 on visas they had obtained through the Aristides de Sousa Mendes, In Portugal. Dali and Gala were to remain in the United States for the next eight years. Here, Dali helped to develop New York as a leading art center and spent a great deal of time writing. He published *The Secret Life of Salvador Dali* in 1942, and wrote scathing attacks on traditional Surrealism, which in his own works, he pushed to the limit. His novel, *Hidden Faces*, followed in 1944, while his relationship with Buñuel broke down irrevocably. During the post-war years, he returned to his native Spain and worked with trompe l'oeil (French for "deceive the eye"), optical illusions, and negative space, as well as experimenting in pointillism. He worked in other mediums and was to become an important influence in pop art. He possessed a natural intelligence and was interested in science and math, which became regular themes in his works from the 1950s onward. While his knowledge of physics was somewhat limited, he was particularly interested in geometry, which led to his great love of the rhinoceros horn – a logarithmic spiral – and DNA. Religion continued to play a part in his life and he returned to Catholicism – hence the Catholic marriage ceremony he celebrated with his wife in the 1950s.

Dali had a fascination for nuclear physics. Interestingly, he had a glass floor featured in his home, which allowed him to work within the parameters of foreshortening and optical illusions. In 1960, he began work on his Dali Theater-Museum in Figueres – the largest single project he had ever undertaken, which he worked on up to and including the 1980s. When Dali was 77, Gala died and the artist's world was turned upside down. He became dehydrated deliberately (to what purpose is unclear) and moved to the castle in Pubol where Gala had died. After a fire broke out in the castle, he moved back to Figueres where he spent his final years living in his Theater-Museum. Dali already had a pacemaker when he was admitted to hospital with heart failure in 1988. He died on January 23, 1989, and was buried in the Theater-Museum, situated just a few blocks from the house where he was born.

Great Works

Paintings

Accommodations of Desire
(1929)

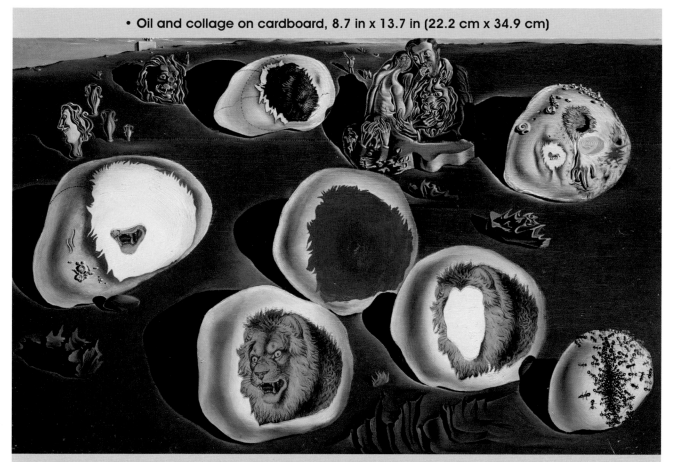

• **Oil and collage on cardboard, 8.7 in x 13.7 in (22.2 cm x 34.9 cm)**

Dali, Salvador (1904-1989): The Accommodations of Desire, 1929. Digitale New York, Metropolitan Museum of Art. Oil and cut-and-pasted printed paper on cardboard, 8 3/4 x 13 3/4 in (22.2 x 34.9 cm). Jacques and Natasha Gelman Collection, 1998. Acc.n.:1999.363.16.Photo: Malcolm Varon.
© 2013. Image copyright The Metropolitan Museum of Art/Art Resource/Scala, Florence © Salvador Dali, Fundació Gala-Salvador Dalí, DACS, 2013.

Dali created the piece *Accommodations of Desire* in the summer of 1929, the same year that he fell in love with Gala Éluard. The autobiographical painting expresses his sexual neuroses and, in particular, his anxieties about his love affair with an older, married woman. In early interviews, Dali describes the painting as an explanation of his relationship with his domineering father, and his father's disapproval of his relationship with Gala. At the top of the painting a naked man, supposedly a self-portrait of Dali, clings to an older man. A lion merges into him; Dali previously used the image of a lion to represent his father. Another man hangs his head in shame, and according to Dali, this is another self-portrait. Seven enlarged pebbles, each containing a precognitive image, illustrate the artist's fears. A toupee, a colony of ants, and ferocious lions are featured in the painting.

Agnostic Symbol

(1932)

• Oil on canvas, 21.3 in x 25.7 in (54 cm x 65.2 cm)

This unusual painting is of an elongated spoon stretched across the desert. It appears from the top right and seems to be traveling endlessly in an almost perfectly straight line, perhaps imitating a beam of light. It curves around a large rock that is in its path before continuing on its journey. In the scoop of the spoon there is a small red clock reading 6.04. The explanation behind the painting is thought to be expressing the idea of bent light, warped space, and suspended time.

Apotheosis of Homer (Diurnal Dream of Gala)

(1944-1945)

• Oil on canvas, 25.2 in x 46.1 in (63.7 cm x 116.7 cm)

Dali, Salvador (1904-1989): Apotheose des Homer – Tagtraum von digitale Gala. 1944/45. Munich, Sammlung Moderne Kunst in der Pinakothekder Moderne, Bayerische Staatsgemaeldesammlungen. Sammlung ModerneKunst. Leinwand. Objektmaß Leinwand. Inventar-Nr.: 14253
© 2013. Photo: Scala, Florence/BPK, Bildagentur fuer Kunst, Kultur und Geschichte, Berlin © Salvador Dali, Fundació Gala-Salvador Dali, DACS, 2013.

Recalling his paranoiac-critical approach that he favored in many of his 1930s works, Dali's creation *Apotheosis of Homer* resonates the true Surrealist style, while adding the intricacy of classicism and realism.

The dreamlike scene features the sleeping body of Gala on a shore, previously seen in *Dream Caused by the Flight of a Bee around a Pomegranate One Second before Awakening*, surrounded by both chaotic and eloquent imagery. Dali said that the painting is a detailed narration of the world of blind people.

The head and shoulders of a man propped up with a crutch blend flesh and stone, and in place of the eyes, a stony platform exists. From the mouth, the angel of speech emerges. The canvas presents intricate detail, from the water droplets on the cracked stone floor to the various objects suspended in mid-air. In the foreground, two snakes entwined around a crossbow are carved into a large slab of gray rock. Also etched into the rock above the carving is Hebrew lettering. Interestingly, the word makes no real sense and there has been some speculation as to whether the letters are an encryption.

In the background, ferocious wild horses cantering in from the sea pull a chariot in which a semi-naked man appears to be whipping the horses.

This beautiful piece hangs in the Modern Museum of Art in Munich.

Apparition of Face and Fruit-Dish on a Beach
(1938)

• Oil on canvas, 45 in x 56.6 in (114.3 cm x 143.8 cm)

Dali, Salvador (1904-1989): Apparition of Face and Fruit-Dish on Digitale (4)(A)a Beach. 1938. Hartford (CT), Wadsworth Atheneum Museum of Art. Oil on canvas. 45 x 56 5/8. The Ella Gallup Sumner and Mary Catlin Sumner Collection Fund. 1939.269 © 2013. Wadsworth Atheneum Museum of Art /Art Resource, NY/Scala, Florence
© Salvador Dali, Fundació Gala-Salvador Dalí, DACS, 2013.

In 1938, Dali broke away from the Surrealist group following political and philosophical differences and disagreements with the movement's founder and leader, André Breton. Despite leaving the group, Dali continued to hone his paranoiac-critical method. This technique is adopted for Dali's creation *Apparition of Face and Fruit-Dish on a Beach*. At first glance, the onlooker may see the female face at the center of the painting, the fruit dish laden with pears, or the brown and white dog in the top right corner. The piece depicts dozens of commonplace objects that, together, create multiple illusions. While some of the images are articulate and detailed, others remain elusive and vague, adding to the dreamlike scene that the piece creates. Each fragmented element blends into a new image: the dog's collar is made up of a bridge, the beach itself becomes the table on which the fruit dish is sat.

Autumnal Cannibalism

(1936)

• Oil on canvas, 25.6 in x 25.6 in (65.1 cm x 65.1 cm)

Autumn Cannibalism, 1936. Artist: Salvador Dali Autumn Digitale Cannibalism, 1936. Painted just after the outbreak of the Spanish Civil War in Spain, this work shows a couple locked in a cannibalistic embrace. Found in the Tate collection, London. 2013. Photo Art Media/Heritage Images/Scala, Florence © Salvador Dali, Fundació Gala-Salvador Dali, DACS, 2013.

The backdrop of this famous painting is the Spanish Empordà plain, which Dali features in many of his 1930s works. *Autumnal Cannibalism* was created in the same year as *Soft Construction with Boiled Beans (Premonition of Civil War)*, and the power of the imagery created clearly reflects the unstable times that Dali was living in. Upon a table, two warped beings simultaneously feast upon each other's bodies. Although the image itself, along with the painting title, conjures up a disturbing scenario, the man and woman in the painting are enjoying their feast politely, delving into the flesh with cutlery.

Locked in embrace, the man's hand squeezes milk from the woman's breast into a bowl while the woman's arm curls around the man's neck, her hand slicing at his flesh with a knife. Their heads are melted together and supported by a crutch. Ants crawl around the space where the woman's mouth should be. Upon the table, two slabs of uncooked meat and a loaf of bread lie untouched.

Crucifixion (Corpus Hypercubicus)
(1954)

• Oil on canvas, 76.5 in x 48.8 in (194.4 cm x 123.9 cm)

Salvador Dali arrived back from America at La Havre in March 1953, announcing that he was to create the first painting whose conception is genuinely based on cubist elements unfolding in the fourth dimension. The piece he created was a striking interpretation of the crucifixion, with Mary Magdalene stood before the suspended cross. The intricate and flawless attention to detail of her robes gives the piece a very realistic quality often seen in the works of Baroque artists Velázquez and Zurbarán, both of whom influenced Dali in this piece.

Dream Caused by the Flight of a Bee around a Pomegranate One Second before Awakening

(c. 1944)

• Oil on wood panel, 20.1 in x 16.1 in (51 cm x 41 cm)

Dali, Salvador (1904-1989): Dream caused by the Flight of a Bee around a Pomegranate One Second before Awakening, 1944. Madrid, Museo Thyssen-Bornemisza. Oil on panel. 51 x 41 cm. Dimension with frame: 73 x 63 x 9 cm. Inv. N.: 1974.46 © 2013. MuseoThyssen-Bornemisza/Scala, Florence © Salvador Dali, Fundació Gala-Salvador Dali, DACS, 2013.

Inspired by a dream Gala supposedly had featuring a bee flying around a pomegranate, Dali created this piece as a fantastical dream sequence. Calm waters and light on the horizon set the scene in which Gala is the subject, suspended several inches above ground in a seemingly peaceful sleep.

The floating droplets of water, along with the naked woman levitated above the flat rock, suggest that time itself has been suspended momentarily.

The elephant strides across the background on fragile spindly legs with an obelisk on its back. The insect-type legs suggest that the enormous animal is weightless, while the obelisk symbolizes power and domination. This image of the elephant later appears in the painting *The Temptations of St. Anthony*.

Two pomegranates are featured in the painting – the first hovers beside Gala with a bee flying close to the fruit. The second pomegranate creates the fantastical scene with a fish leaping from within the fruit from which a tiger bursts out of its mouth. A second tiger dives from the mouth of the first in a threatening stance along with a rifle with fixed bayonet. It is thought that the tigers symbolize the bee with their yellow and black stripes, while the bayonet represents the stinger of the insect.

The painting displays sexual suggestions in several areas: the pomegranate is a Christian symbol of love, fertility, and resurrection, while the bee is an insect that traditionally symbolizes the Virgin.

Family of Marsupial Centaurs

(1940)

• Oil on canvas, 14 in x 12.2 in (35.6 cm x 31 cm)

Dali, Salvador (1904-1989). The Family of Marsupial Digitale Centaurs; La Famille des Centaures Marsupiaux. 1940. London, Private Coll. oil on canvas. 35.6 x 31 cm
© 2013. Christies' Images, London/Scala, Florence © Salvador Dali, Fundació Gala-Salvador Dali, DACS, 2013.

This painting, *Family of Marsupial Centaurs,* is undoubtedly removed from the typical works of Dali, who announced in the 1940s that he was turning to classicism. This complex genius has certainly found a classical tone in this possibly little-known piece. The Spanish Surrealist was obsessed with his time in the womb and, in fact, even claimed that he could remember it and was fully aware of his own experiences. He was fascinated by the trauma of birth and, here, chooses not to explore humans, but the mythical creatures from Greek mythology: centaurs, with their horse bodies and human heads. The centaurs take on a marsupial-type role where the young are able to leave the "pouch" and return freely. It's an unusual work, with its coastline similar to those Dali had left behind in his native homeland. However, this canvas was completed during the Second World War while he and Gala were in exile. The painting is constructed in such a way that there is a visible "X" that touches all four corners and separates four equal sections where each are strong in their own right. Notice particularly the meticulous attention to detail, so typical of Dali.

Gradiva Rediscovers the Anthropomorphic Ruins (Retrospective Fantasy)

(1931-1932)

• Oil on canvas, 25.6 in x 21.3 in (65 cm x 54 cm)

Dali, Salvador (1904-1989): Gradiva Rediscovers the Anthropomorphic Ruins (Retrospective Fantasy), 1932. Madrid, Museo Thyssen-Bornemisza. Oil on canvas. 65 x 54 cm. Dimension with frame: 79 x 67.5 x 4 cm. Inv. N.: 1975.39. © 2013. Museo Thyssen-Bornemisza/Scala, Florence © Salvador Dali, Fundació Gala-Salvador Dali, DACS, 2013.

Created during Dali's Surrealist years, this painting was inspired by the novel *Gradiva* by Wilhelm Jensen. The story became the basis of Sigmund Freud's study for "Delusion and Dream in Jensen's Gradiva." The story is of an archeologist who becomes obsessed with a bas-relief woman he sees in a museum. Upon returning to his home in Germany he dreams that he is transported back in time where he meets the real woman from the bas-relief walking through the streets of Pompeii while the hot ashes of Vesuvius cover the city. This dream prompts the archeologist to return to Italy on a quest to find the woman he believes to be the reincarnation of Gradiva.

To Dali, Gradiva was Gala and he uses the figure in several of his paintings. In this piece, the foreground image of a human form in stone represents Gradiva. Colored in dark shades, the figure displays cracks in the stone and holes where the face, heart, and genitals should be. An inkwell sits upon her shoulder, which some art historians believe to be a reference to Dali's father's office.

Illuminated Pleasures

(1929)

• Oil and collage on composite panel, 9.4 in x 13.7 in (23.8 cm x 34.7 cm)

Dali, Salvador (1904-1989): Illuminated Pleasures, 1929. New York, Museum of Modern Art (MoMA). Oil and collage on composition board, 9 3/8 x 13 3/4 in. (23.8 x 34.7 cm). The Sidney and Harriet Janis Collection. 584.1967 © 2013. Digital image, The Museum of Modern Art, New York/Scala, Florence © Salvador Dali, Fundació Gala-Salvador Dalí, DACS, 2013.

Although small, this piece contains a great deal of detail and again explores the realms of the unconscious mind. As with dreams, the chaotic images don't appear to make rational or logical sense. The backdrop for this painting is one that is familiar in many of Dali's works: a bleak desert with blue skies.

The foreground images include three boxes, each containing its own mini scene. The largest box centered in the painting makes reference to *The Great Masturbator*, in which Dali includes a self-portrait seen from the earlier painting. Above the face, a grasshopper is poised. Dali uses the image of a grasshopper in several other paintings. It is an insect that he fears, and he uses it in his work to symbolize destruction, waste, and fear. A naked man peers into the side of this box as though spying on the events that occur within.

The box to the left depicts a man in a suit shooting at a spherical object, with a historical building (possibly a church) in the background. The detail in this section of the piece delivers incredible realism while appearing almost photographical. The final box, placed to the right, features dozens of men on bicycles, each with a spherical object on their head.

At the bottom of the piece, a hand holding a bloody knife is raised, while another hand grasps around the wrist of the first, possibly trying to prevent further destruction. A woman with bloodstained hands desperately tries to escape a man that is holding her captive, his hand wrapped around her throat. A shadow of a human is visible, as though someone witnesses the distressing scene of her struggle, or perhaps they are taking in the entire scene of the dream before them.

It is a complex piece that once again demonstrates the Freudian influence in Surrealist paintings.

Sleeping Woman, Horse, Lion
(1930)

- Oil on canvas, 23.9 in x 27.7 in (60.6 cm x 70.4 cm)

Dali, Salvador (1904-1989). Dormeuse, Cheval, Lion Digitale Invisibles. 1930. London, Private Coll. oil on canvas. 60.6 x 70.4 cm. © 2013. Christies' Images, London/Scala, Florence
© Salvador Dalí, Fundació Gala-Salvador Dalí, DACS, 2013.

Dali gave the following definition of *Sleeping Woman, Horse, Lion*: "The double image (the example of which may be that of the image of the horse alone which is at the same time the image of a woman) can be prolonged, continuing the paranoiac process, the existence of another obsessive idea being then sufficient to make a third image appear (the image of a lion, for example) and so forth, until the concurrence of a number of images, limited only by the degree of the capacity for paranoiac thought." The work was completed in Port Lligat in the summer of 1930 and was a piece that Dali often wrote about. The work was exhibited in the gallery of Pierre Colle and was bought by the Viscount of Noailles. It was an important experimental piece in terms of Dali's double images, with its reference to the persistence of desires. It is an exceptionally clever piece – one of three paintings on the same subject, although the works had different titles and one was destroyed during demonstrations in Paris on December 3, 1930.

Madonna

(1958)

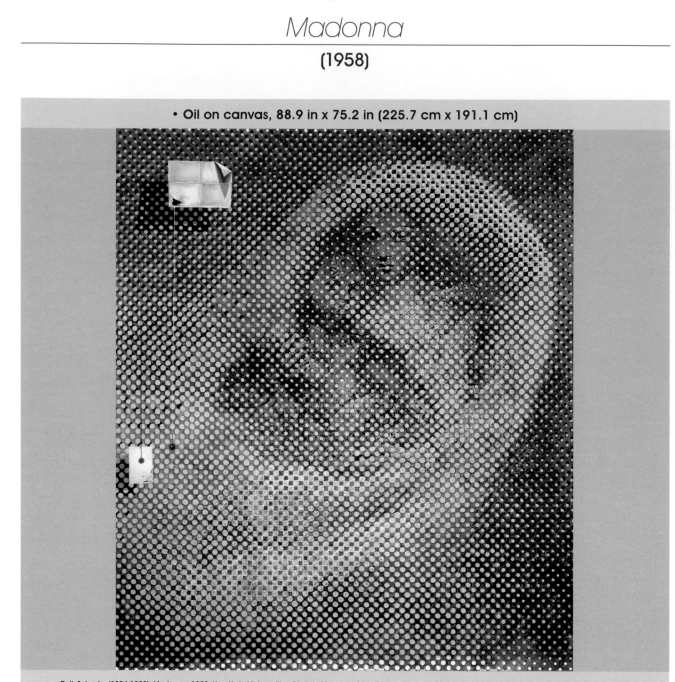

• Oil on canvas, 88.9 in x 75.2 in (225.7 cm x 191.1 cm)

Here, Dali paints two subjects in a series of gray and pink dots. The *Madonna* consists of classical imagery on which Dali has based his Surrealism. The work contains the Madonna and child, and a large ear. Completed during his Surrealism epoch, the Madonna and child painting has its basis in Raphael's *Sistine Madonna* (1613), and the two figures define the presence of the large ear. The ear takes its form from a newspaper photograph of the then pope's ear – Pope John XXIII. The motifs are designed to come into focus at different distances. For example, at close range the picture gives the impression of being abstract. From a much greater distance, the large ear – what Dali termed "the ear of an angel" – is the prominent feature. However, at a moderate distance from the work, the Madonna and child become the main focus. A forward-thinking man with vision, Dali anticipated the pop art of the future and uses the Benday dots in a fantasy effect, with an oversize pattern of halftone dots. On the "surface" of the work, Dali includes trompe l'oeil objects – the technique of using realistic imagery to create an optical illusion that depicts that objects exist in three dimensions – comprising a suspended cherry, which projects a shadow onto a piece of paper containing the artist's signature, and a further piece of paper from which the cherry hangs on the string.

Moment of Transition

(1934)

- **Oil on canvas, 20.9 in x 25.6 in (53 cm x 65 cm)**

Dali, Salvador (1904-1989). Moment de Transition. 1934. Digitale London, Private Coll. oil on canvas. 53 x 65 cm. © 2013. Christies' Images, London/Scala, Florence
© Salvador Dali, Fundació Gala-Salvador Dalí, DACS, 2013.

Moment of Transition echoes Dali's earlier piece, *The Phantom Cart,* which he painted in 1933. Using a similar palette to the previous piece, hues of yellows, oranges, and browns are used to create the desert-like landscape. The addition of dark, craggy rocks and mountains gives this piece a slightly different feel to the vast, bleak landscape of *The Phantom Cart.*

A solitary woman, dressed all in white, walks across the desert toward the traveling cart, while another figure stands watching the cart approaching them. The horse and cart form part of the buildings that lay ahead, as previously demonstrated in *The Phantom Cart.*

Partial Hallucinations
(Six Images of Lenin on a Grand Piano)
(1931)

• Oil on canvas, 44.9 in x 57.5 in (114 cm x 146 cm)

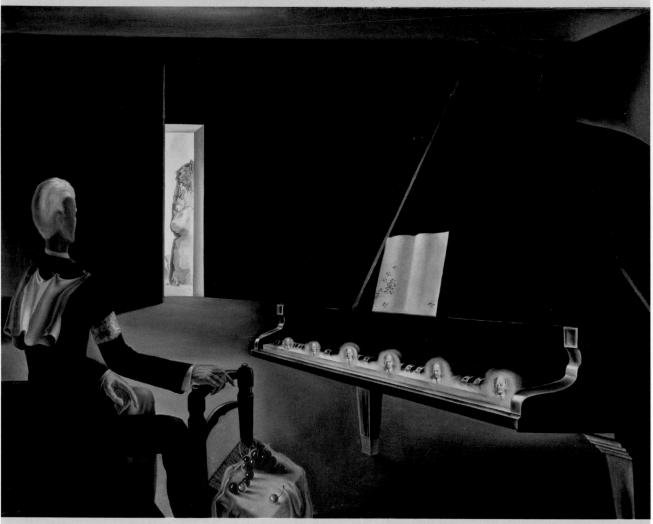

Dali, Salvador (1904-1989): Hallucination partielle: six apparitions de Lenine sur un piano. 1931. Paris, Musee Nationald'Art Moderne – Centre Pompidou. Peinture
© 2013. WhiteImages/Scala, Florence © Salvador Dali, Fundació Gala-Salvador Dalí, DACS, 2013.

Partial Hallucinations features some of the typical elements that Dali uses frequently in his work. In the painting, a white-haired man is seated facing a grand piano, his hand resting on the back of a wooden chair before him. Upon the chair lies a white cloth filled with cherries. Two further cherries are attached to the man's arm.

A blank music sheet is upon the piano on which dozens of ants crawl. On the piano keyboard, six faces of Lenin appear to be hovering in yellow phosphorescent orbs. To the rear of the otherwise empty room, a door opens to show a rocky landscape beyond.

Dali spoke of his source of inspiration for this painting, saying that images came to him before going to bed one night. "At sunset, I saw the bluish, shiny keyboard of my piano, where the perspective exposed to my view a series in miniature of little yellow phosphorescent halos surrounding Lenin's visage."

It is thought that the painting portrays Dali's father, mourning the loss of his first son. Dali later used cherries in his painting *Portrait of My Dead Brother* in 1963 whereby the precise placing of the fruit forms the face of a young boy. In this painting Dali mimicked a similar technique adopted by American pop artist Roy Lichtenstein.

Pierrot with Guitar

(c. 1923)

• Oil and collage on cardboard, 21.5 in x 20.6 in (54.5 cm x 52.3 cm)

Dali, Salvador (1904-1989): Pierrot with a Guitar. c. 1923. Madrid, Museo Thyssen-Bornemisza. Oil and collage on cardboard, 54.5 x 52.3 cm INV. Nr. 512 (1986.12).
© 2013. Museo Thyssen-Bornemisza/Scala, Florence © Salvador Dali, Fundació Gala-Salvador Dalí, DACS, 2013.

One of Dali's early works, *Pierrot with Guitar* demonstrates use of oil and collage techniques. The fragmented elements of the piece clearly illustrate Dali's early interest in Cubism. *Pierrot with Guitar* is heavily influenced by Pablo Picasso – through the use of techniques employed and the subject matter. Two years after creating the piece, Dali visited Paris with his sister, Ana Maria, and his stepmother, Catalina, for the first time. It was during this visit that he finally met his hero Picasso, and for the young Dali this was an incredible experience. He later recalled: "When I arrived at Picasso's on Rue de la Boëtie, I was as deeply moved and full of respect as though I was having an audience with the pope."

Portrait of Luis Buñuel

(1924)

• Oil on canvas, 27.6 in x 23.6 in (70 cm x 60 cm)

Dali, Salvador (1904-1989): Portrait of Luis Bunuel, 1924. digitaleMadrid, Museo Nacional Centro de Arte Reina Sofia. Oil on canvas. ©2013. DeAgostini Picture Library/Scala, Florence
© Salvador Dali, Fundació Gala-Salvador Dalí, DACS, 2013.

Salvador Dali first met Luis Buñuel at the Royal Academy of Arts in Madrid In 1922. He became a great inspiration to the young artist and later became an important force in Dali's life. Together they worked on the Surrealist movie *Un Chien andalou* in 1929, and *L'Age d'or* in 1930.

In this piece, Dali uses a post-Impressionist style of heavy color and thick brush strokes to capture the serious and authoritative image of Luis Buñuel. The use of somber colors adds to the solemn look on the subject's face.

This portrait became important to Dali as it was one of the pieces that increased recognition of his talent and of his work. *Portrait of Luis Buñuel* was the first of his paintings to be exhibited outside of Catalonia.

Portrait of Mrs. Isabel Styler-Tas
(1945)

• Oil on canvas, 25.8 in x 33.9 in (65.5 cm x 86 cm)

Dali, Salvador (1904-1989): Portrait of Mrs. Isabel Styler-Tas Digitale (6)(A)(Melancholy), 1945. Berlin, Nationalgalerie, Staatliche Museen zu Berlin. Oil on canvas, 65.5 x 86 cm. Inv.: B 359. Photo: Joerg P. Anders. © 2013. Photo Scala, Florence/BPK, Bildagentur fuer Kunst, Kultur und Geschichte, Berlin © Salvador Dali, Fundació Gala-Salvador Dalí, DACS, 2013.

Mrs. Isabel Styler-Tas was a patron of Dali's while he was in the United States. His portraiture work was not widely regarded as favorably as his other paintings, and in this oil, Mrs. Styler-Tas's mirror image is portrayed on the left in a deathly reverse. Dali realized that working in portraiture, however, was a lucrative business. With his fame on the increase, this realization manifested itself during the 1940s at a time when his work in advertising, movie theaters, and fashion drove him as a leading European artist. He was not short of wealthy clientele and he made himself available to them. Here, he has included dreamscapes and Surrealism, themes he was to include in other portraits. It isn't a particularly striking or flattering portrait of the lady in question, yet it has essential qualities that draw the audience to the piece. Perhaps the lack of flattery is exactly why it does, with its "ice cold" lady who appears to have a dead animal perched on her head. The woman is not portrayed as beautiful – yet it is unlikely that Isabel Styler-Tas thought herself ugly – and her mirror image is just as unflattering. The road into the "head" seems to go nowhere, except to the empty sky, while her profile is formed in the image of rocky crags. It is a fairly "dead" mirror image. The piece is almost certainly cynical in its approach. Yet, it's clear from the detail and intensity of the work that Dali put a great deal of effort into the painting – it is truly reminiscent of the man who was "inspired," above all, by art.

Portrait of Mrs. Jack Warner

(c. 1945)

• Oil on canvas, 43.7 in x 37.2 in (111.1 cm x 94.6 cm)

Dali, Salvador (1904-1989). Portrait of Mrs. Jack Digitale (A)Warner. 1945. London, Private Coll. oil on canvas. 111.1 x 94.6 cm © 2013. Christies' Images, London/Scala, Florence © Salvador Dali, Fundació Gala-Salvador Dalí, DACS, 2013.

Having found themselves exiled in the United States, Dali and Gala settled in California, where Hollywood beckoned in 1944. Dali was already internationally recognized as a leading European artist, and America was keen to cash in on the talents and foresight he had to offer. Alfred Hitchcock and Walt Disney both wanted to work with him: he created the dream sequence for Hitchcock's *Spellbound* and worked on Disney's animated short film *Destino*. Jack Warner, the movie magnate, was also particularly taken with Dali. It is well known that the two men had a mutual respect and understanding and shared a quick wit that no doubt added to their relationship. Dali was a "name" that the social elite were keen to become associated with. Dali painted his portrait of Jack Warner's wife around 1944/45, following in his established tradition of Surrealist portraitures. This piece is almost a photographic likeness of the subject, surrounded by a Surrealist setting of a bizarre landscape and sky. Like the "road to nowhere" in the portrait of Mrs. Isabel Styler-Tas, the bridge in this work also appears to have no purpose. Mrs. Warner is resting her arm on what many describe as a possible classical sarcophagus. The work is fairly unconventional and shows the wife of Jack Warner staring blankly into the distance. Warner was so impressed by this work that he commissioned his own portrait after Dali had finished. There is some discrepancy with regard to when this work was actually completed. Here, we have dated the painting in the mid-1940s – as noted by some experts – however, in some circles, this work has been traditionally dated to 1951.

Soft Construction with Boiled Beans (Premonition of Civil War)

(1936)

• Oil on canvas, 39.4 in x 39 in (100 cm x 99 cm)

Dali, Salvador (1904-1989): Soft Construction with Boiled Beans (Premonition of Civil War). 1936. Oil on canvas, 39 5/16 x 39 3/8 in (99.9 x 100 cm). The Louise and Walter Arensberg Collection, 1950. Philadelphia, Philadelphia Museum of Art. © 2013. Photo: The Philadelphia Museum of Art/Art Resource/Scala, Florence
© Salvador Dali, Fundació Gala-Salvador Dali, DACS, 2013.

Dali created this famous painting to represent the horrors of the Spanish Civil War, however, the piece was completed six months before General Franco led a military coup against the democratically elected government of the Second Spanish Republic. There had been political and social struggle in the country for several years.

There has been some speculation about the title, and it is thought that Dali added "Premonition of Civil War" at a later date. The piece was first shown in London, in 1936, under the title *Soft Construction with Boiled Apricots* when it was incorrectly translated. The image was then reproduced for the magazine *Minotaure* under the title *Spain, Premonition of Civil War*. It wasn't until 1937, when the piece was shown in the United States for the first time at the international exhibition at the Carnegie Institute in Pittsburgh, that it was displayed with its current title.

Although the painting is dated 1936, Dali began sketching ideas for *Soft Construction with Boiled Beans* in 1934. The image that dominates the painting is that of a grotesque creature aggressively tearing its limbs apart. The face of the monstrous being is contorted into a grimace of torture and pleasure. Dali employs his paranoiac-critical method to force the limbs of the monster into an outline of the map of Spain. He creates a contrasting landscape by painting a beautiful Catalonian sky against a bleak and desert-like terrain, which he refers to as being the Empordà plain of north Catalonia. The area, which is usually green and fertile, has been transformed into the lifeless desert, representing the harsh effects of war.

Boiled beans are scattered on the ground in the painting and Dali is quoted to have said, "One could not imagine swallowing all that unconscious meat without the presence of some mealy and melancholy vegetable."

While the painting expresses the atrocities of war and the destruction it brings, Dali did not openly side with the Republic or the fascist regime and preferred to remain apolitical. The Civil War greatly affected Dali: his sister, Ana Maria, was captured and tortured by the communist soldiers fighting for the Republic, and his friend, Federico Garcia Lorca, was murdered by a fascist firing squad.

The Angelus of Gala (Portrait of Gala)

(1935)

• **Oil on wood panel, 12.8 in x 10.5 in (32.4 cm x 26.7 cm)**

This exciting work shows the artist's wife in a double image, just as if she were regarding herself in a mirror. The main figure in the painting is seated on a cube with her back to the audience, while slightly to the left is the much smaller forward-facing image. The forward-facing image is gazing at herself, however, she is not seated on the cube, but on a wheelbarrow, which reflects the painting hanging on the wall behind her. The symmetry of the mirror image is shattered by the change, but adds to the beauty and mystery of the work. The oil on wood is based on the well-known work by Jean-François Millet, the 19th-century French artist, of *The Angelus*, which depicts a peasant man and a woman standing next to a wheelbarrow, in an empty field, praying over a basket of potatoes. The painting had hung in the classroom of the school that Dali had attended and was well known to him, if disturbing. It is widely known that Dali believed that the basket contained the coffin of a child and that the woman was being portrayed as a praying mantis. It is a painting to which Dali made numerous references in his works of the early 1930s. It was a developing paranoid creative process where the images he portrayed were infused with hidden images. However, when looking at Millet's painting, to an alternative audience, the work describes in detail the Catholic devotion time. Millet had been born to peasant parents in Cherbourg in the 19th century, a time when men and women worked the land but were called to stop and pray when the church bell rang. It was a three-time daily ritual, and here we see the man and his wife stopping for the Angelus after hearing the bell from the church in the distance. Yet, to Dali, rather than being a calm, rational painting, which depicted how life was for French peasants, he sees a work that literally fueled his obsessions and fears. For Dali, Millet's work showed a "monstrous example of disguised sexual repression," and not two humble peasants living their daily lives.

Dali's *The Angelus of Gala* contains two versions of *The Angelus*. The unsymmetrical portrait of the double Gala is one version, while *The Angelus* hanging on the wall behind the second Gala is the other. The forward-facing Gala, while gazing, is almost staring aggressively at her double. It is not an attractive depiction of the artist's wife and it is cited that the aggressive look on her face is a reflection of Dali's interpretation of the peasant woman – a praying mantis – in the Millet work. It is suggested that the first Gala – the figure with her back to the audience – is the male counterpart, yet this may not be the case. In nature, the female would be considerably larger than the male. To have them the other way around, when Dali believed that the female was about to devour her partner, in Millet's painting, does not really fit with the idea of paranoiac fears.

The Enigma of Desire or My mother, my mother, my mother (L'Enigme du Desir or Ma mere, ma mere, ma mere)

(1929)

• Oil on canvas, 43.5 in x 59.3 in (110.5 cm x 150.5 cm)

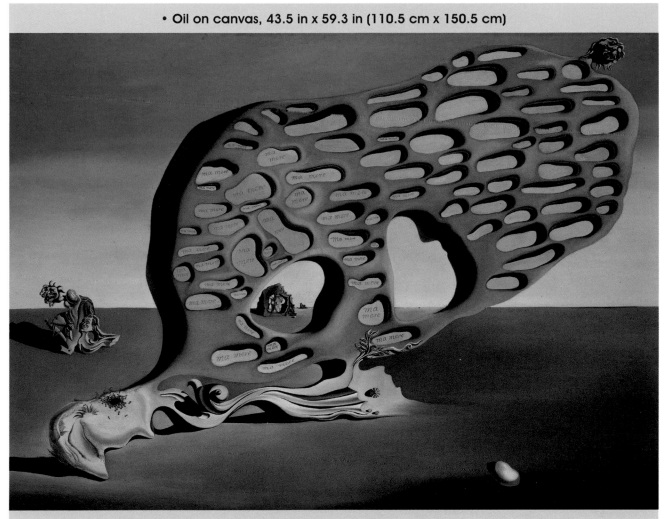

Dali, Salvador (1904-1989): Das Raetsel der Begierde (LŽEnigme du Digitale Desir) – oder Ma mere, ma mere, ma mere, 1929. Munich, Sammlung Moderne Kunst in der Pinakothek der Moderne, BayerischeStaatsgemaeldesammlungen. Leinwand Oel, Inv.: 14734© 2013. PhotoScala, Florence/BPK, Bildagentur fuer Kunst, Kultur und Geschichte, Berlin © Salvador Dali, Fundació Gala-Salvador Dalí, DACS, 2013.

Considered by Dali to be one of his 10 most important paintings, *The Enigma of Desire* was created in his aunt's dressmaking workroom following the summer of 1929. It was the first work sold by Goemans Gallery during Dali's first one-man exhibition there in 1929. Recalling his childhood home in Figueres, the landscape depicts the desolate and seemingly infinite Ampurdán plain. The painting itself features images that recur in other works, including a human face that appears in *The Great Masturbator*, which was created at the same time as *The Enigma of Desire*, and one of Dali's most recognized works, *The Persistence of Memory*. The abstract face has been used in several of his works to represent Dali himself as an unusual self-portrait.

On the cheek of the face Dali has included the cluster of ants, also featured in many other works. His fascination with the tiny insects began in childhood, where he would watch in awe, as despite their size, colonies of these small creatures would devour an entire animal. The use of ants in his work represents death, decay, and a metaphor for change.

The expansive rock-like formation that connects to the face resembles the coastal rocks of Cadaqués, again reminiscent of Dali's landscapes from youth. The surface of the rock is covered with the words "Ma Mere," French for "My Mother." A small group to the left illustrates Dali locked in an embrace with his father, a fish, a grasshopper, and a lion's head.

The Enigma of Desire can be described as a mournful tribute to his mother, using a range of elements to express his complex feelings toward her.

The Enigma of William Tell

(1933)

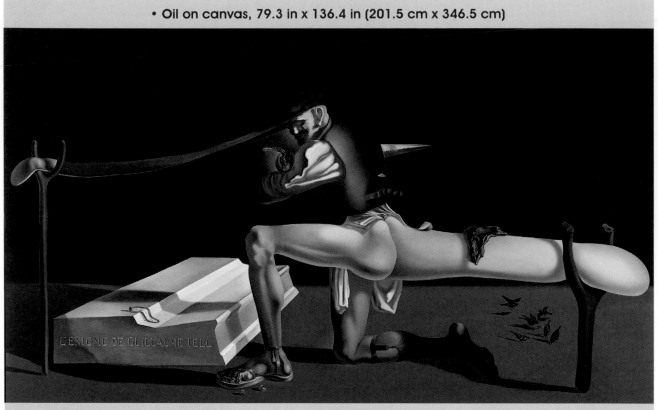

• Oil on canvas, 79.3 in x 136.4 in (201.5 cm x 346.5 cm)

L'ENIGME DE GUILLAUME TELL

Dali, Salvador (1904-1989): The Enigma of William Tell, 1933. digitale Stockholm, Moderna Museet. Oil on canvas. © 2013. DeAgostini PictureLibrary/Scala, Florence
© Salvador Dali, Fundació Gala-Salvador Dalí, DACS, 2013.

This painting, which today hangs in the Modern Museum in Stockholm, Sweden, is particularly strange. It is a powerful and provocative work with an impossibly exaggerated elongation of the figure's right buttock propped up by a classic Dali crutch. Another crutch holds the equally elongated brim of the figure's hat. The figure is that of Lenin, and the menacing image is intended as a symbol of the artist's estrangement from his father. The difficult relationship between father and son was common in Dali's works as a means of exploring and expressing the fragile, obsessive, and disturbing. Dali Senior had been especially disapproving of his son's relationship with Gala and had been abhorred that the couple lived together before marriage. The buttock in this work is undoubtedly phallic and surreal, and caused an outcry amongst other Surrealist artists who supported Marxist idealism. The sardonic portrayal of Lenin led to some of Dali's peers attempting, unsuccessfully, to destroy the work. Breton, Benjamin Péret, and Yves Tanguy attempted to deface the work as it hung at the Grand Palais, but it was too high for them. Dali's relationship with Breton began to flounder at this time and he was almost expelled from the Surrealist movement for this radical portrayal of Lenin.

Here, Dali used the legend of William Tell as a metaphor, but instead of there being an apple on the boy's head, there is a raw piece of meat (a lamb cutlet). Lenin (or the father figure) is holding the child. The cannibalistic implication cannot be lost here; Dali described it as "the symbol of passionate, cannibalistic, ambivalence." Gala is also represented in the painting – as a tiny baby image poised near Lenin's left foot (which emphasizes "father as destroyer"), who, in turn, kneels before an altar. Upon this, Dali had painted the title of the work and included a famous soft watch. The painting is both unusual and almost comic with regard to its elongations. Dali, while profound and complex, had an acute sense of humor.

This was the most famous of Dali's William Tell trilogy. The crutches are intended to symbolize death and resurrection, while the altar is shaped like a piano – a common theme for the artist at this time.

The Lacemaker After Vermeer

(1954)

Dali, Salvador (1904-1989): The Lacemaker (after Vermeer), Digitale (7)(A) Spanish, 1955. New York, Metropolitan Museum of Art. Oil on canvas, 9 1/4 x 7 3/4 in (23.5 x 19.7 cm). Signed (upper right): Dali Inv. N.: 1975.1.232 © 2013. Image copyright The Metropolitan Museum of Art/Art Resource/Scala, Florence
© Salvador Dalí, Fundació Gala-Salvador Dalí, DACS, 2013.

This exquisite work was Dali's interpretation of Vermeer's *Lacemaker,* a copy of which had hung in his father's study. Dali's obsession with the painting had materialized as early as 1928 in his Surrealist silent movie, *An Andalusian Dog.* By the 1950s, Dali was experimenting with the molding of religion and science in order to prove the existence of God. The painting was created during his "Atomic Period," and while his beliefs on physics were completely misguided, he did give some thought to geometry. He was obsessed with the rhinoceros, the horn of which is in the form of a logarithmic spiral. It is a biologically recognized pattern, controlled by different growth rates in various parts of the horn. In the case of the rhinoceros, it results in a curved horn. A "candy-cane" spiral results in a narwhal, and Dali was renowned for using both in his works. He discusses this in *50 Secrets of Magic Craftsmanship,* which he wrote in 1948. He agreed that all curved surfaces on the human body could be decomposed into logarithmic spirals.

Dali was commissioned to paint the work by Robert Lehman, an art collector, who had struggled in vain to obtain his own Vermeer. Dali studied the original in the Louvre and made several copies of the work, including a deconstruction with rhino horns. The face in Dali's version is much more harsh than the original, note the "spiky" nose, but it's unclear whether this painting was completed as depicted in the mid-1950s, or earlier. However, he completed up to 50 copies of the Vermeer painting, and with the Lehman work turned what was a "peaceful" portrayal into something altogether much more bold and with different meanings. He elevates the rhino and the *Lacemaker* into a vision of chastity, but noted that the *Lacemaker* was dominant; for Dali, she was morphologically a rhinoceros horn.

The Old Age of William Tell
(La Vieillesse de Guillaume Tell)

(1931)

• Oil on canvas, 38.6 in x 55.1 in (98 cm x 140 cm)

In 1930, Salvador Dali had a terrible row with his father, which became the theme of a series of paintings in this era. In addition to his father's disapproval over his son's relationship with Gala, Dali was heard saying "sometimes I spit on the picture of my mother for the fun of it," a remark that contributed to the heated argument between father and son.

The legend of William Tell is a story about a bowman who refuses to acknowledge authority. As punishment, he is forced to shoot an arrow through an apple placed on his son's head. In *The Old Age of William Tell* there is no obvious link to the myth of William Tell, although Dali uses the story to relate the exploration of the relationship he has with his father.

The painting explores fear, shame, and sexual desire. The formidable dark shadow of a lion prowls in front of a sheet, representing Dali's father. Behind the sheet, two women perform sexual acts upon a gray-haired man; two figures are locked in a passionate embrace to the left, while a young couple is turned away in shame with hands upon their faces. It has been suggested that these symbolize Adam and Eve cast out from the Garden of Eden, and this can be strongly linked to the artist's feelings about himself and Gala. At the bottom of the piece a dying rose signifies Dali's dying love for his father.

In Dali's book *Diary of a Genius* he quotes Freud: "The hero is the man who resists his father's authority and overcomes it." The artist felt that the break between father and son was inevitable and subsequently beneficial for him.

The Persistence of Memory

(1931)

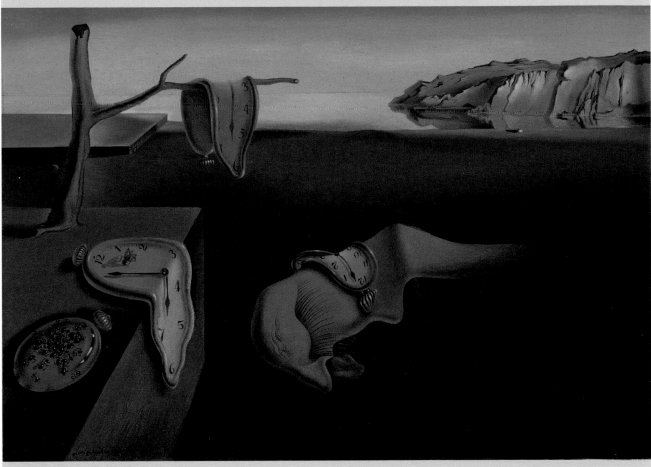

• Oil on canvas, 9.5 in x 13 in (24.1 cm x 33 cm)

Dali, Salvador (1904-1989): The Persistence of Memory (La Digitale persistence de la memoire), 1931. New York, Museum of Modern Art(MoMA). Oil on canvas, 9 1/2 x 13 in (24.1 x 33 cm). Given anonymously. Acc. n.: 162.1934.© 2013. Digital image, The Museum of Modern Art, New York/Scala, Florence
© Salvador Dali, Fundació Gala-Salvador Dalí, DACS, 2013.

The Persistence of Memory is undoubtedly one of Salvador Dali's most famous and recognizable works. Like many of his pieces, Dali uses his Catalonian surroundings to inspire the location for his subject. The landscape in this painting resembles an area near Port Lligat, the craggy rocks in the distance reminiscent of Cap de Creus.

The vaguely human face at the center of the painting is once again present as a distorted self-portrait of the artist that reappears frequently in other pieces, including *The Great Masturbator* and *The Enigma of Desire*. The eyes are closed and heavily lashed, indicating that the being is asleep.

Four clocks, three of which are melting, appear in this piece. The fourth is a closed red pocket watch crawling with ants, the insects focusing on the center of the object. Each of the melting clocks display a different time.

Many art historians have speculated that *The Persistence of Memory* could be a visual explanation to Albert Einstein's theory of relativity – the melting clocks representing the idea that time is not fixed. However, Dali's interest and research into Sigmund Freud's theories lend a far more psychoanalytical approach to his work.

The Persistence of Memory has long since been open to interpretation, ranging from the elusive to the meaningful. Many have thought that the melting clocks are a metaphor for Dali's fear of impotency. One suggestion is that time is irrelevant during sleep, and since Dali expressed the ideas of the unconscious mind and dreams in various other pieces during the 1930s, this explanation could be fairly accurate.

When Dali was asked about his source of inspiration for the piece, he answered that it was a Surrealist perception of Camembert melting in the sun.

The Phantom Cart

(1933)

• Oil on wood panel, 6.3 in x 8.6 in (15.9 cm x 21.9 cm)

Two versions of this painting exist, both created in 1933. Once again, Dali utilizes his paranoiac-critical method in *The Phantom Cart*. Using monochromatic colors, the cart is seen traveling away into the distance of a vast desert in the Mediterranean coastal region.

As the title suggests, the cart and passengers aboard also lend themselves to the architecture of the town beyond, implying that its ghostly visage plays two parts in the painting. The cart also appears in *Moment of Transition*, which Dali painted the following year.

The Spectral Cow (La Vache Spectrale)

(1928)

• Oil on plywood, 19.7 in x 25.4 in (50 cm x 64.5 cm)

This painting dates back to the time when Dali had not fully discovered his own style and was beginning to explore the realm of Surrealism. It is one of the early indicators as to what artistic path he would follow. Surrealist artists would often depict poetry in their work, and in this painting Dali is exploring André Breton's collection of poems, *Clair de Terre*.

The cow to the left is merely suggested in the piece, its body formed in a series of outlines. The textures appear both jagged and feathered in places with various colors used. To the right there is a ghostly form of a bird with only its legs visible. Upon the richly colored shore, another smaller cow or sheep is present with a hollowed-out section where the eye should be.

Dali went on to create another piece in the same year called *The Ram (The Spectral Cow)*, where a ram with an empty circle for its eye faces a bird.

The Spectre and the Phantom
(1934)

• Oil on canvas, 39.4 in x 28.7 in (100 cm x 73 cm)

Dali, Salvador (1904-1989). The Spectre and the Phantom; Digitale Le Spectre et le Fantome. 1934. London, Private Coll. oil on canvas. 100 x 73 cm.
© 2013. Christies' Images, London/Scala, Florence © Salvador Dali, Fundació Gala-Salvador Dalí, DACS, 2013.

The work comes in a series of paintings covering the theme of spectral appearances and phantoms. Dali describes the theme here as the clouds and rainbow taking the part of the specter and the brick-shape as taking the form of the phantom in a letter he wrote to Paul Éluard. The work was part of the artist's paranoiac-critical method and has the same female figure as *Mediumistic-Paranoiac* (1935), sitting in the foreground. She is seated in a puddle on a beach. The woman is based on three figures, including Dali's nurse, his loyal friend, Lidia, and the man who became one of his obsessions, Adolf Hitler. The soft flesh of Hitler's back had become an obsession, held in by its tight uniform, and he had dreamt of the Nazi leader as a wet nurse sitting, knitting in a puddle. The woman in this painting has a cut taken out of her back, emphasizing Dali's thoughts on the issue.

The Transparent Simulacrum of the Feigned Image
(1938)

• Oil on canvas, 28.5 in x 36.2 in (72.4 cm x 92.1 cm)

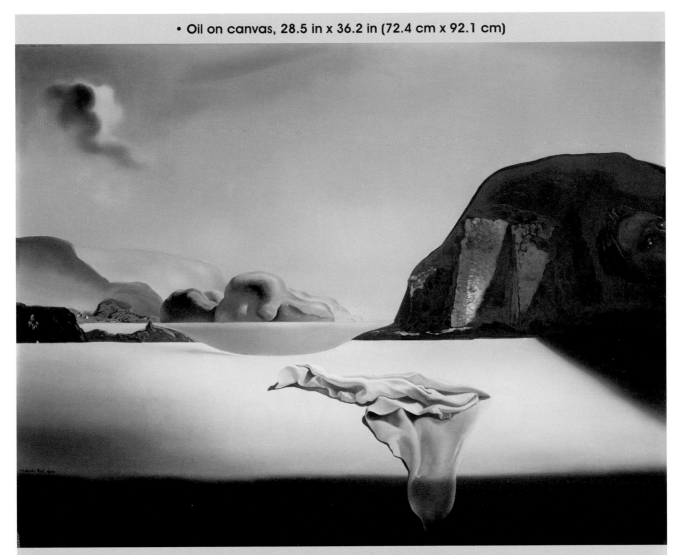

Dali was particularly interested in dreams and dreaming – the fact that objects, time, and space could be so readily distorted – and he believed that dreams were a way that the unconscious mind chose to deal with the realities of living. He worked on the idea that thoughts were unraveled and expressed in dreams and related to the people, things, and places that surround each and every individual. This work was created to expose the anxiety that can be felt in dreams, but he wanted it to convey the fascinating magic and mystery that accompany them. Dali was renowned for his use of double images, and this work is no exception. It successfully incorporates a table on top of which are a napkin and a bowl of food; however, these images also represent a bay (the bowl) and mountains in the distance (its contents), thereby demonstrating a landscape as the second subject. The title of this work suggests that nothing is as it seems – a see-through, semblance of something, not real, perhaps in something visual, or something in the mind. To the right edge of the painting is a floating head, representing Gala, as the support and inspiration that she played in his life. Actually, something very real. This work, as were many others, is signed by both Dali and Gala, a further nod to the crucial part Gala played in Dali's existence.

Great Works

Other Works

Cleo-catra
(1946)

• Pen, India ink, and watercolor over pencil on board, 4.9 in x 4.5 in (12.4 cm x 11.4 cm)

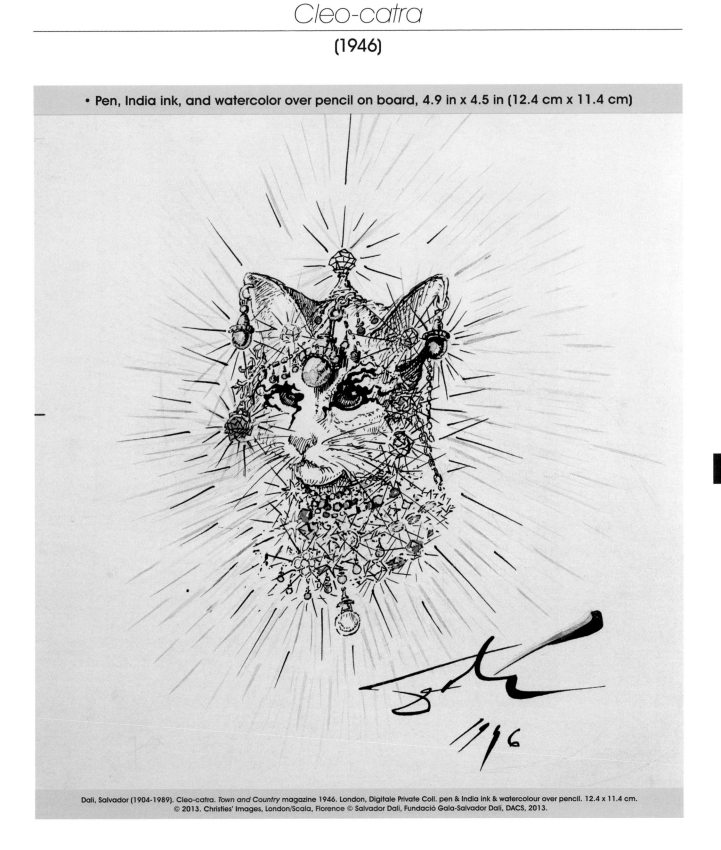

Dali, Salvador (1904-1989). Cleo-catra. *Town and Country* magazine 1946. London, Digitale Private Coll. pen & India ink & watercolour over pencil. 12.4 x 11.4 cm.
© 2013. Christies' Images, London/Scala, Florence © Salvador Dali, Fundació Gala-Salvador Dali, DACS, 2013.

Cleo-catra is an exotic image of Cleopatra portrayed as a feline. The pen, India ink, and watercolor work was created in 1946 and given as a gift to Lincoln Kirstein of New York. It was eventually auctioned by Sotheby's for $36,000. In 1946, this exciting work was included in an issue of *Town and Country* magazine.

Cover of the magazine *Minotaure*

(1936)

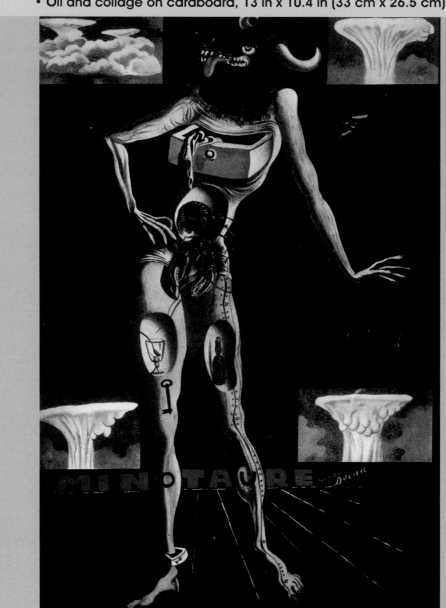

Dali, Salvador (1904-1989): Cover of the magazine *Minotaure*. © 2013. White Images/Scala, Florence © Salvador Dali, Fundació Gala-Salvador Dalí, DACS, 2013.

Minotaure was a Surrealist-orientated magazine published between 1933 and 1939. It became one of the richest sources of information for Surrealist artists and writers before its collapse in 1939 through lack of funding and the outbreak of the Second World War. It was an incredibly important source for Dali during his most creative period, and many of his works – both written and artistic – were featured in the magazine.

This cover design was used for the eighth issue of *Minotaure*, and is typical of the artist's work during his paranoiac-critical method era. Using a restrictive palette of black, gray, red, and flesh tones, the image depicts long naked legs of a woman connecting to a hollowed-out torso, where a lobster is emerging. An open drawer fills the space where the woman's breasts should be, and the head of a beast takes the place of a human head.

Dali uses the idea of drawers coming out of a body in several other pieces, including *The Anthropomorphic Cabinet*, *Venus de Milo*, and *Burning Giraffe*.

Hidden Faces

(1945)

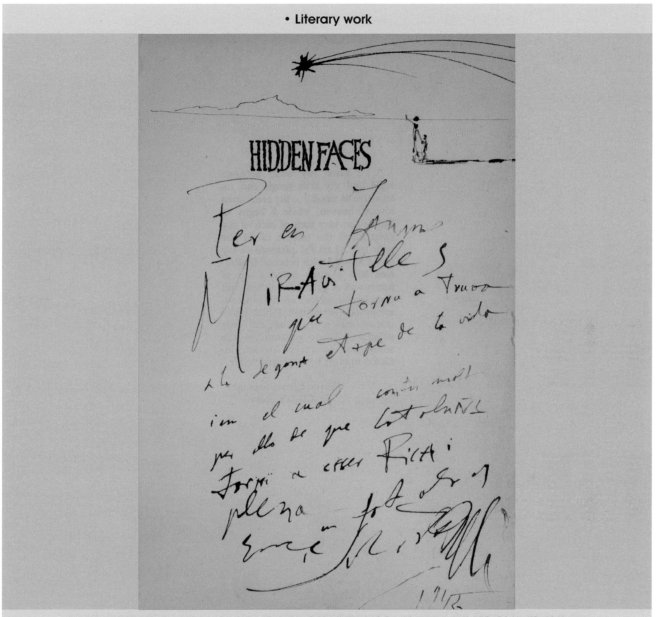

Dali, Salvador (1904-1989): Hidden Faces. 1945. Buffalo (NY), Digitale (5) Albright-Knox Art Gallery. Ink on paper, sheet: 7 7/8 x 5 1/4 in. (20 x 13.33 cm.).
Gift of Dr. and Mrs. Clayton Peimer, 1986.© 2013. Albright Knox Art Gallery/Art Resource, NY/Scala, Florence © Salvador Dali, Fundació Gala-Salvador Dali, DACS, 2013.

Hidden Faces, written by the artist in 1945, was Dali's only novel. In it, he describes the loves and lives of a group of characters – from the aristocracy – who symbolized European decadence in the 1930s. It outlines their luxurious lives, their extravagances, and the beauty with which they were surrounded, from the riots in Paris in 1934 to the end of the Second World War. It clearly outlined the artist's ideas in rich language, which brings together all the themes in his art. The book contains Dali's own drawn illustrations.

He was fascinated by the Arcimboldo technique, created by the Italian painter, Giuseppe Arcimboldo, who used various fruits, vegetables, books, fish, and other objects to create impressive painted portraits on canvas. His own paranoiac-critical method was influenced by Arcimboldo. He felt the technique was a form of self-concealment, "I wear a mask," and he used it to great effect in his novel, as well as many of his great paintings. He writes quite differently to the way in which he expressed his art; critics have reviewed the book as being an exceptional, witty, and perhaps, although still bizarre in the usual Dali way, not as much as some of the paintings.

Retrospective Bust of a Woman

(1933) (some elements reconstructed in 1970)

• Porcelain, corn, bread, feathers, inkwell, beads, sand, and two pens

Dali, Salvador (1904-1989): Retrospective Bust of a Woman (Bustede femme retrospectif), 1933. New York, Museum of Modern Art (MoMA). Painted porcelain, bread, corn, feathers, paint on paper, beads, ink stand, sand and two pens, 29 x 27 1/4 x 12 5/8 in. (73.9 x 69.2 x 32 cm). Acquired through the Lillie P. Bliss Bequest and gift of Philip Johnson (by exchange). 301.1992 © 2013. Digital image, The Museum of Modern Art, New York/Scala, Florence © Salvador Dali, Fundació Gala-Salvador Dalí, DACS, 2013.

Despite his earlier view that Surrealist sculptures were "absolutely useless," Salvador Dali became increasingly interested in the idea of making surreal *objets*, inspired by leader of the Surrealist group, André Breton. His childhood dream of becoming a chef motivated the use of food in sculptures. His 1936 creation *Lobster Telephone* would later become an iconic Surrealist sculpture in 20th-century art.

Retrospective Bust of a Woman features the nude porcelain bust of a woman, carrying a French baguette and bronze inkwell on her head. The latter was inspired by Millet's painting *The Angelus*, a piece that had interested Dali for many years.

Around the woman's neck she wears a pair of maize cobs. The piece presents the idea that the woman is more than just an object: like the food that adorns her, she too is to be consumed. Ants gather on her brow and at her lips as though searching for crumbs.

In 1933 the sculpture was shown at the Salon sur indépendants, where Picasso's dog is said to have eaten the original loaf of bread. When Dali made his first trip to America, he arrived in New York wearing a baguette on his head, mimicking his own creation.

St. George and the Dragon

(1947)

Etching on woven paper, 28.6 in x 15.2 in (72.7 cm x 38.7 cm)

Dali, Salvador (1904-1989): St. George and the Dragon, 1947. New York, Museum of Modern Art (MoMA). Etching, plate: 17 5/8 x 11 1/4 in. (44.8 x 28.6 cm); sheet: 22 7/16 x 15 3/16 in. (57 x 38.6 cm). Larry Aldrich Fund. Acc. n.: 248.1952.© 2013. Digital image, The Museum of Modern Art, New York/Scala, Florence © Salvador Dalí, Fundació Gala-Salvador Dalí, DACS, 2013.

Dali was fond of grandiose heroics and this etching from 1947 shows his keenness for the theme in one of his most compelling graphic works. The turmoil outlined in this work is captured through the art of etching and showcases Dali as a creative draftsman, with its strong, "carved" lines. It is one of the few pieces on which Dali signs his full name.

Dali

In The 21ˢᵗ Century

■ **ABOVE:** This photo, *Telephone aphrodisiaque*, 1938, by Salvador Dali, is displayed in front of a screen showing an interview of the artist during the presentation to the press of the Dali exhibition at the Centre Pompidou Modern Art Museum in Paris at a retrospective of Salvador Dali in Paris, 2012.

(AP Photo/Francois Mori) © Salvador Dali, Fundació Gala-Salvador Dalí, DACS, 2013.

■ **ABOVE:** The *Mae West Room* at the Centre Pompidou Modern Art Museum, Paris.

■ **OPPOSITE:** Sculpture, *The Triumphant Angel*, resides on the top floor of the Soumaya Museum's new home in Mexico City.

Dali's legacy lives on and will continue to do so throughout the 21st century. There is speculation that art dealers today are wary of later Dali works because there were rumors that before the artist died, he was forced by his guardians to sign blank canvases. However, the genuine works of this refreshing and complex man are highly sought after. Over the past few years, there have been many exhibitions dedicated to the paintings and other mediums in which Dali worked, the world over. One of the most enduring legacies from Dali must surely be the Dali Theater-Museum in Figueres, which is the largest Surrealist object in the world. It occupies the site of the former Municipal Theater. Although started in 1960, the museum was inaugurated in 1974 and contains a broad range of works spanning the artist's career. Included in the museum's collection are *The Girl from Figueres* (1926), as well as *Soft Self-Portrait with Fried Bacon* (1941), and *Dawn, Afternoon and Evening* (1979), while the pieces that were created specifically for the site include the *Mae West Room*, and the *Monument to Francesc Pujols*. Dali carefully designed every aspect of the museum so that visitors could really experience the artist and his works to full advantage. Dali was instrumental in the smallest of details in the construction of the museum, and the transparent grid structure – a geodesic dome – which crowns the building, (from an original idea by the artist himself), is one of the most exciting elements of the building.

The Gala-Dali Foundation manages various collections of Dali's work, which consists of literally thousands of objects and more than 4,000 works of art encompassing all the mediums that Dali worked in. This includes paintings, drawings, sculptures, engravings, jewelry, holograms, installations, movies, photography, and fashion. Many of these are on permanent display at the museum, and parts of the collections are available for temporary exhibitions at other worldwide institutions.

Dali Universe was a permanent exhibition of art works held in County Hall in London. It opened in 2000 and closed in January 2010 – where it was intended it would open at a new location, to be confirmed. The exhibition housed more than 500 works including sculptures, drawings, glass, and lithographs. Part of the exhibition is now on show at the Dali Universe, Venice. This exhibition has more than 100 artworks and important sculptures (including *Space Elephant*). There are also rare graphics, which illustrate great literary themes, as well as glass objects. The exhibition – Dali Universe – was organized by Beniamino Levi, who has been responsible for more than 80 Dali exhibitions. There are many museums and galleries dedicated to Dali, including the Salvador Dali Gallery in California and the Salvador Dali Museum in St. Petersburg, Florida, as well as the Espace Dali in Paris.

(AP Photo/Dario Lopez-Mills) © Salvador Dali, Fundació Gala-Salvador Dalí, DACS, 2013.

(AP Photo/Katsumi Kasahara)

■ **ABOVE:** Visitors form a long queue outside Tokyo's Ueno-no-Mori Art Museum, 2006. Since its opening, the Centennial Retrospective Dali exhibition has attracted many visitors.

Useful books

Salvador Dali by Rachel Barnes and Salvador Dali (Dec. 10, 2009)

Salvador Dali – The Paintings (2 Vol) by Robert Descharnes and Gilles Neret (Sep. 25, 2007)

Dali (Taschen Basic Art Series) by Catherine Plant (May 26, 2000)

The Secret Life of Salvador Dali by Salvador Dali and Haakon M. Chevalier (Sep. 10, 2010)

Diary of a Genius by Salvador Dali (Mar. 1, 2007)

Dali (Taschen Basic Art Series) by Gilles Neret (Oct. 25, 2011)

Salvador Dali: The Making of an Artist by Catherine Grenier (Nov. 19, 2012)

Salvador Dali (Critical Lives) by Mary Ann Caws (Nov. 10, 2008)

Hidden Faces by Salvador Dali (Jul. 5, 2007)

Dali and the Path of Dreams by Anna Obiols and Joan "Subi" Subirana (Apr. 1, 2007)